The Intermediate Excel Quiz Book

M.L. HUMPHREY

SELECT TITLES BY M.L. HUMPHREY

EXCEL ESSENTIALS
Excel for Beginners
Intermediate Excel
50 Useful Excel Functions
50 More Excel Functions

EXCEL ESSENTIALS QUIZ BOOKS
The Excel for Beginners Quiz Book
The Intermediate Excel Quiz Book
The 50 Useful Excel Functions Quiz Book
The 50 More Excel Functions Quiz Book

DATA PRINCIPLES
Data Principles for Beginners

EASY EXCEL ESSENTIALS
Pivot Tables
Conditional Formatting
Charts
The IF Functions
Formatting
Printing

CONTENTS

INTRODUCTION

This is a companion book written to complement *Intermediate Excel* by M.L. Humphrey and is geared towards those who are already familiar with the content covered in that book who now want to test their knowledge through quizzes or to those who learn better from a question and answer format.

For each chapter in *Intermediate Excel* there is a set of questions meant to test your knowledge of the information that was covered in the chapter.

The first section of the book just has the questions, the next section of the book has the questions as well as the answers. There is also a bonus section that contains five exercises where you can test your knowledge of the various functions by applying them to specific real-life scenarios.

I encourage you to try to do each exercise first without looking at the solutions, since in the real world you'll be faced with a problem that needs solved and no one will be there to tell you how to solve it. However, I would also encourage you to have Excel open as you work each exercise so you can use the help functions within Excel to find what you need. Don't feel like you need to memorize every task in Excel in order to use it effectively. You just need to know what's possible and then what keywords or phrasing to use to help you find the information that will let you perform the right task.

Alright, then. Let's start with the first quiz.

QUIZZES

CONDITIONAL FORMATTING QUIZ

1. What does conditional formatting allow you to do?

2. Where can you find the Conditional Formatting option?

3. What conditional formatting options are available in Excel 2007?

4. If you want to mark all cells that have a value greater than $3,500, what conditional formatting option should you use?

5. If you want to mark all cells that have a value less than $1,500, what conditional formatting option should you use?

6. If you want to mark all cells that contain a certain text phrase, what conditional formatting option should you use?

7. If you want to flag when a value occurs more than once, what conditional formatting option can you use?

8. What is the issue with using the Duplicate Values conditional formatting option?

9. How can you customize the format that's applied to a range of cells when using conditional formatting for the greater than and less than rules?

10. If you want to flag the top 10 values in your range of data, which conditional formatting option can you use to do that?

11. Is it possible to flag just the top 5 values? If so, how?

12. What if you want to flag the top 10% of your results using conditional formatting, how can you do that?

13. Can you flag any % of your results?

14. How would you flag results that are above the average value for the range using conditional formatting?

15. How would you flag results that are below the average value for the range using conditional formatting?

16. What do Data Bars do?

17. What do Color Scales do?

18. What do Icon Sets do?

19. Can you customize the limits Excel uses when applying data bars, color scales, and icon sets? How?

20. How can you remove conditional formatting from a range of cells?

21. What if you only want to remove one conditional formatting rule from a range of cells, how can you do that?

22. How do you change the order in which conditional formatting rules are applied to a cell or range of cells?

23. What other option do you have for adding a new conditional formatting rule to your data other than using one of the pre-defined options (Highlight Cells Rules, Top/Bottom Rules, etc.)?

INSERTING SYMBOLS QUIZ

1. How do you insert a symbol into a cell in Excel?

2. Can you insert a symbol into a cell that already has text in it?

3. Which font has a lot of images like scissors, mailboxes, smiley faces, etc?

4. If you need the copyright symbol or trademark symbol, where can you find those?

5. Can you change the size or color of a symbol you've inserted? If so, how?

6. Once you've inserted a symbol into a cell can you change the font without impacting the symbol?

PIVOT TABLES QUIZ

1. What does a pivot table allow you to do?

2. How do you need to format your data in order to use a pivot table?

3. What are some best practices when formatting your data for analysis?

4. How do you start a pivot table?

5. Should you add your pivot table to your existing sheet or to a new one? Why?

6. What are the two ways you can add a field to your blank pivot table?

7. If you drag a field to the Filters section, what can you do with that field?

8. If you drag a field to the Rows section, how will that field appear in the table?

9. If you drag a field to the Columns section, how will that field appear in the table?

10. If you drag a field to the Values section, how will that field appear in the table?

11. How can you change the function that is performed on a field that you've placed in the Values section?

12. What functions can you apply to a field in the Values section?

13. If you want to format the values in your table, what are two ways to do so?

14. Can you perform two or more calculations on the same field in a pivot table? If so, how?

15. Can you have multiple fields for your rows or columns?

16. What would be the drawback in doing so?

17. Can you filter which results show for your rows or columns fields? For example, if you just wanted to see one customer's results in the rows section, could you do that? How?

18. Can you reorder the fields in the rows or columns section?

19. How can you get the PivotTable tools menu options to display?

20. What does the Group tool do under Analyze under PivotTable Tools?

21. How do you do this?

22. How do you remove a grouping?

23. If you do have a set of results grouped, how do you see the totals for that group?

24. If you have a set of results grouped and are only able to see the summary for the group, how do you make the individual results visible?

25. If you have multiple groups that you want to collapse to the summary level, how can you do this?

26. If you have multiple groups that you want to expand at once, how can you do this?

27. What does the Slicer do?

28. How do you reset any fields you've filtered using the Slicer?

29. What does Insert Timeline let you do?

30. What does Refresh do?

31. Why is Refresh useful?

32. What issue could you run into using Refresh that you need to be careful about?

33. What option can you use to change the data that's being used in your pivot table?

34. When might you want to change your data in your pivot table?

35. What should you watch out for when updating your data source?

36. What option can you use to clear your currently selected fields from your pivot table and return to a blank pivot table?

37. What option can you use to just clear any filters you've applied to your pivot table?

38. If you want to calculate the value of one field in your table times another field in your table, what's the best way to do this? Where is that option located?

39. What does the Design tab under PivotTable Tools allow you to do?

40. Name two ways you can remove a field you've added to a pivot table that you decide you don't want.

41. How can you change the order of the fields when you have multiple fields for Row, Column, or Value?

42. Can you write formulas that reference cells within a pivot table?

43. If you have generated a pivot table and want to use that data elsewhere but don't want to risk having the data update on you, what can you do?

44. Is it advisable to create a pivot table and then do calculations on the values of that pivot table outside of the table while leaving it in pivot table format? Why or why not?

SUBTOTALING AND GROUPING DATA QUIZ

1. What does the Subtotal option let you do?

2. Where is the Subtotal option located?

3. What must you do before you can subtotal your data?

4. What will happen if you try to subtotal unsorted data?

5. How do you subtotal data?

6. Which field in the Subtotal dialogue box is for the field you want to separate your data by?

7. Is this the only field Excel will perform the subtotal function on?

8. Can you perform different functions on different fields when you subtotal?

9. What functions can you choose to perform using subtotal?

10. How do you choose which fields to apply the function to?

11. Does the field you subtotal by also have to be a field you apply a function to?

12. Can it be?

13. What will checking the box for "page break between groups" do?

14. What will checking the box for "summary below data" do?

15. Once you've subtotaled your data, what do the numbers at the left-hand side of the row numbers do?

16. How do you remove subtotals?

17. What if you want to keep the subtotals you created, but just remove the grouping options on the left-hand side of the worksheet?

18. What does the Group option allow you to do? Where is it located?

19. When might you use this?

20. How do you group a set of rows or columns?

21. What is one requirement for any set of rows or columns you want to group?

22. If you've successfully grouped a set of rows or columns, how will you know?

23. How can you hide a set of grouped columns or rows?

24. How can you reveal a set of grouped columns or rows that are currently hidden?

25. How can you remove all grouping from a worksheet?

26. Should you use Ctrl + Z and Ctrl + Y when using subtotaling or grouping?

CHART TYPES QUIZ

1. What makes charts so useful?

2. How should you configure your data for most charts?

3. Once you have your data input in Excel, how can you create a chart of it?

4. How can you preview what your chart will look like?

5. What is time series data?

6. Which chart options are best for use with time series data?

7. For data with multiple variables (such as multiple vendors) but no time component (so 2018 summary, for example), what are the best chart options to use?

8. What are scatter plots good for?

9. What is the difference between a column chart and a bar chart in Excel?

10. What does a clustered columns graph do?

11. What are the advantages/disadvantages of a clustered column graph?

12. What does the stacked columns graph do?

13. What are the advantages/disadvantages of a stacked columns graph?

14. What does the 100% stacked column graph do?

15. What are the advantages/disadvantages of a 100% stacked column graph?

16. Is there generally a reason to use 3-D graphs in your presentations?

17. What is a pie chart?

18. What is the difference between a pie chart and a doughnut chart?

19. What does a pie of pie chart do?

20. What does a bar of pie chart do?

21. Which is generally better to use if you must use one, the pie of pie chart or the bar of pie chart?

22. What should you do with your data before using a scatter plot with lines in Excel? Why?

23. What is the difference between a scatter plot that uses smooth lines and one that uses straight lines?

24. What is the difference between a scatter plot with markers and one that doesn't have them?

25. Can you plot more than one set of results on a scatter plot at once? How?

EDITING CHARTS QUIZ

1. If the chart you just created has the wrong data points in the wrong places (so maybe it's showing vendor along the axis instead of month), what's one way you can attempt to fix that?

2. If you accidentally included a summary row in your chart, how can you easily fix that?

3. If you want to add another data point, for example, a new vendor to your existing graph, how can you do that?

4. If you want to expand the data points that are included in your chart, how can you do that?

5. How can you change the order in which the elements in your chart display?

6. How can you change your chart type?

7. What are Chart Styles?

8. How can you apply a Chart Style to a chart?

9. Do you have to select a Chart Style to see what it will look like with your data?

10. Does a Chart Style have to be exactly what you want for you to use it?

11. What is a Quick Layout?

12. How can you apply a Quick Layout to your chart?

13. Do you have to click on a Quick Layout option to see what it will look like on your chart?

14. Can you further customize a chart after you've applied a Quick Layout to it?

15. Can you use both a Chart Style and Quick Layout on the same chart? If so, what challenges are there to doing so?

16. What's the easiest way to change the colors in your chart?

17. What chart elements can you add or delete from a chart?

18. Where can you go under Chart Tools to add chart elements to your chart?

19. What does the Axes option allow you to do?

20. What does the Axis Titles option allow you to do?

21. When you use Axis Titles, is the title for that axis already populated?

22. What does Chart Title allow you to do?

23. What does Data Labels allow you to do?

24. When can Data Labels be particularly useful?

25. What does Data Table allow you to do?

26. What does Gridlines let you do?

27. What does Legend do?

28. What does Trendline allow you to do?

29. How can you change the size of your chart?

30. How can you move a chart to a new position within your worksheet?

31. How can you move a chart to a new worksheet or other document?

32. How can you manually rearrange the elements within a chart, such as the chart title?

33. Can you move all elements in a chart?

34. How do you change the title of a chart?

35. How do you change the name of a data field that's displayed in the legend of your chart?

36. How can you apply custom colors to your chart elements?

37. When should you use Shape Fill?

38. When should you use Shape Outline?

39. What do you need to be careful of when applying custom colors to your chart?

40. If you mess up, what's the easiest way to fix it?

41. What does the Formatting Task Pane do?

42. If you want to have the segments in your pie chart separated to make them more clearly visible, where can you go to do this?

43. Can you use the Home tab Font options to edit the font color, size, or style in a chart?

REMOVING DUPLICATE ENTRIES QUIZ

1. If you have a column that has duplicate values and you want to narrow the list down to just unique values, how can you do that?

2. In the Remove Duplicates dialogue box, what does checking the "my data has headers" box do?

3. When you have Excel remove duplicates from a single column of data what happens to that data?

4. Can you remove duplicate values across multiple columns?

5. How does that work?

6. Can you remove duplicates from two out of six columns in a data range? Should you?

7. Why should you always do any calculations or manipulations on a copy of your source data instead of the original copy?

CONVERTING TEXT TO COLUMNS QUIZ

1. What does Text to Columns allow you to do?

2. What is the most basic use of Text to Columns?

3. Before you apply Text to Columns to a column of data what should you do?

4. If I have a list of entries in Column A that are first name space last name, so "Mark Jones", "Dave Clark", etc. how can I separate that list into two columns, one with first name and one with last name and with no extra spaces?

5. If I have a list of entries in Column A where each entry starts with a two-digit number that indicates the year and is followed by a five-digit customer ID, how can I separate the two-digit year into one column and the five-digit ID into another column?

6. When you use the Delimiter option, what happens to your delimiter?

7. How can you delete a break line you placed that you don't want to use?

8. How can you move a break line you placed that isn't in the right location?

9. Can you choose more than one delimiter (say a space and a comma) under the Delimiter option?

10. Can you specify a custom delimiter? How?

11. Can you specify how you're newly-separated data will be formatted? How?

12. What do you need to be careful of when using the Delimiter option with Convert Text to Columns?

13. What function allows you to remove excess spaces from around text?

CONCATENATE QUIZ

1. What does the CONCATENATE function let you do?

2. What is the basic format of a CONCATENATE function?

3. Let's say you have customer first name in Cell A1, customer last name in Cell B1, and that you want to create an entry that's "LastName, FirstName" (last name comma space first name) using those values. How would you write that using the CONCATENATE function?

4. How would you create an entry that's "FirstName Last Name" (first name space last name)?

5. What would the result be from the function =CONCATENATE("Jones",", ","Albert")? What does the ", " portion in the center represent? And why do we need the quotation marks around Jones and Albert?

6. After you've used the CONCATENATE function to create an entry, what do you need to be careful about with respect to the entry you've created?

7. How can you address this issue?

THE IF FUNCTION QUIZ

1. What does an IF function do?

2. Translate the IF function =IF(A2>25,0,A2*0.05) into a written description.

3. What is another way to think about the components of an IF function?

4. What does it mean that you can nest IF functions?

5. If you're going to nest IF functions, which is it better to replace, the Then portion or the Else portion? Why?

6. Translate the IF function =IF(A9>A5,B5,IF(A9> A4,B4,0)) into a written description.

7. If you were to copy the above formula into a new cell, how would it change?

8. If you have a long and complex nested IF function that you can't get to work, what are some ways you can troubleshoot the IF function to figure out what's wrong?

9. What is the most likely issue if Excel tells you you've entered too many arguments with an IF function?

10. What should you always do with an IF function that you create? (Or any function really?)

11. If you write an IF function that's referencing a table of fixed values (like a discount table) what should you always be sure to do?

COUNTIFS QUIZ

1. What does the COUNTIFS function do?

2. How does this differ from the COUNTIF function?

3. Which should you use?

4. What is the following function doing:
   =COUNTIFS(B2:B6,"Alaska")

5. What is the following function doing:
   =COUNTIFS(A1:A10,">25")

6. What is the following function doing:
   =COUNTIFS(C10:C200,"*a*")

7. What is the following function doing:
   =COUNTIFS(C10:C200,"*e")

8. Could any of the above four examples also be written using the COUNTIF function?

9. What is the following function doing:
=COUNTIFS(C10:C200,"Alaska",D2:D200,"Whatsits")

10. Could you use COUNTIF with the above example?

11. What do you need to watch out for in terms of your cell ranges when using multiple count criteria?

12. Can you have a COUNTIFS function that includes a text criteria and a numeric criteria both?

13. If you write a COUNTIFS function that references the values in three separate columns, say Columns A, B, and C, how will Excel look at the data to make its count. For example, with the formula

  =COUNTIFS(A:A,"Alaska",B:B,"Whatsits",C:C,"Paid")

what is Excel going to look at to make its count?

14. If you write a COUNTIFS function that references the values in three separate rows, say Rows 1, 2 and 3, how will Excel look at the data to make its count. For example, with the formula

  =COUNTIFS(1:1,"Alaska",2:2,"Whatsits",3:3,"Paid")

what is Excel going to look at to make its count?

15. What is one thing you can do when setting up a COUNTIFS function to make sure it's working before you expand it to your entire worksheet?

SUMIFS QUIZ

1. What does the SUMIFS function do?

2. How does it differ from the SUMIF function?

3. When was it introduced?

4. If you start by writing a SUMIF function and realize you want to write a SUMIFS function, can you do that?

5. If you have access to both SUMIF and SUMIFS, which should you use?

6. Write a description of what =SUMIFS(A1:A10,B1:B10, "NZD",C1:C10,"") is saying.

7. How would you write a SUMIFS function to sum the values in Column C when the values in Column D are greater than 30 and the value in Column E is Smith?

8. Can you apply SUMIFS to a range of cells (so two columns and two rows) and not just a column or row?

9. If you can, what do you need to make sure of?

TEXT FUNCTION QUIZ

1. What does the TEXT function do?

2. If the value in Cell A1 is 5 and you use =TEXT(A1, "$0.00") what result will you get?

3. If the value in Cell A1 is 5 and you use =TEXT(A1, "#.00") what result will you get?

4. If the value in Cell A1 is 5 and you use =TEXT(A1, "#.#0") what result will you get?

5. If the value in Cell A1 is 5 and you use =TEXT(A1, "#.##") what result will you get?

6. If the value in Cell A1 is 4.235 and you use =TEXT(A1, "$0.00") what result will you get?

7. If the value in Cell A1 is 4.235 and you use =TEXT(A1, "#.00") what result will you get?

8. If the value in Cell A1 is 4.235 and you use =TEXT(A1, "#.#0") what result will you get?

9. If the value in Cell A1 is 4.235 and you use =TEXT(A1, "#.##") what result will you get?

10. What is the difference between using a 0 and a # sign in the above examples?

11. What do you need to watch for when using the # sign for formatting?

12. If the value in Cell A1 is 4.235 and you use =TEXT(A1,"$#.##") & " per unit" what result will you get?

13. How can you take a date from Cell A1 and display its day of the week written fully? For example, Sunday.

14. How can you display its abbreviated day of the week? For example, Sun.

15. How can you isolate what day of the month it is from a date in Cell A1?

16. How can you take a date from Cell A1 and display its month of the year written fully? For example, November.

17. How can you display its abbreviated month of the year? For example, Nov.

18. How can you isolate the number for the month of the year from a date in Cell A1?

19. How can you isolate the year from a date in Cell A1?

LIMITING ALLOWED INPUTS QUIZ

1. What is the issue that you run into if you let users enter data in any way they choose?

2. How can you get around this issue?

3. What issue can you run into if you provide a dropdown menu of choices?

4. What's one way around this?

5. What's one danger of doing this?

6. How can you limit the values someone can input into a cell in Excel (general)?

7. If you want to limit users to a list of accepted text entries, what option should you choose? How do you specify the list?

8. If you want to limit users to only entering whole numbers, what option should you choose?

9. If you want users to be able to enter a decimal number instead, what option should you choose?

10. When limiting a user's input to a number (either whole or decimal), what else do you need to do? And what should you be careful about when doing so?

11. What will happen if you've applied data validation to a cell and a user tries to input an answer that isn't allowed?

12. Can you customize the message that displays? Where?

13. How can you remove data validation from a set of cells?

LOCKING CELLS OR WORKSHEETS QUIZ

1. Is it possible to keep users from editing the contents of cells in a worksheet? If so, how?

2. What do you need to watch out for when locking a worksheet?

3. How can you remove protection from a worksheet?

4. Is it possible to hide the contents of cells in a worksheet as well? How?

HIDING A WORKSHEET QUIZ

1. How can you hide a worksheet?

2. How can you unhide a worksheet?

3. How can you hide a worksheet and keep someone from unhiding it?

TWO-VARIABLE ANALYSIS
GRID QUIZ

1. What does a two-variable analysis grid let you do?

2. What shortcut can you use to make it easy to create a two-variable analysis grid?

3. How can you combine a two-variable analysis grid with conditional formatting?

MORE ANSWERS QUIZ

1. What are three ways that you can find out more information on a topic from within Excel?

2. What's the best way to find a function or learn more about a function you want to use?

3. If you need more information than that, what options do you have outside of Excel?

4. When is it better to use a forum than go to the Microsoft website?

5. What's a nice trick you can use when troubleshooting a function?

6. If you do something you didn't want to do, what's the easiest way to reverse it?

7. What's a best practice if you're building a really complex worksheet or one with lots of moving parts?

8. If you're using dates in your files names why use the YYYYMMDD format to record the date?

QUIZ ANSWERS

CONDITIONAL FORMATTING QUIZ ANSWERS

1. What does conditional formatting allow you to do?

It allows you to apply special formatting to cells that meet the criteria that you specify.

2. Where can you find the conditional formatting option?

In the Styles section of the Home tab.

3. What Conditional Formatting options are available in Excel 2007?

Highlight Cells Rules, Top/Bottom Rules, Data Bars, Color Scales, and Icon Sets.

4. If you want to mark all cells that have a value greater than $3,500, what conditional formatting option should you use?

Highlight Cells Rules, Greater Than

5. If you want to mark all cells that have a value less than $1,500, what conditional formatting option should you use?

Highlight Cells Rules, Less Than

6. If you want to mark all cells that contain a certain text phrase, what conditional formatting option should you use?

Highlight Cells Rules, Text that Contains

7. If you want to flag when a value occurs more than once, what conditional formatting option can you use?

Highlight Cells Rules, Duplicate Values

8. What is the issue with using the Duplicate Values conditional formatting option?

It highlights all cells in the range where a value occurs more than once and doesn't distinguish between different values. So a range of cells with more than one "ABC" and more than one "DEF" would have all cells that contain "ABC" and "DEF" flagged the same. This limits its immediate usefulness.

9. How can you customize the format that's applied to a range of cells when using conditional formatting for the greater than and less than rules?

In the Greater Than or Less Than dialogue boxes there are dropdowns that allow you to choose from six pre-defined formats. At the bottom of that list of formats you can also click on Custom Format which will open a Format Cells dialogue box that allows you to choose any formatting you want to apply to the cells.

10. If you want to flag the top 10 values in your range of data, which conditional formatting option can you use to do that?

Top/Bottom Rules, Top 10 Items

11. Is it possible to flag just the top 5 values? If so, how?

Yes. Use the Top/Bottom Rules, Top 10 Items, but change the number to 5 instead of 10.

12. What if you want to flag the top 10% of your results using conditional formatting, how can you do that?

Top/Bottom Rules, Top 10%

13. Can you flag any % of your results?

Yes. Just use the Top/Bottom Rules, Top 10% option, and change the percentage to the one you want to use.

14. How would you flag results that are above the average value for the range using conditional formatting?

Top/Bottom Rules, Above Average

15. How would you flag results that are below the average value for the range using conditional formatting?

Top/Bottom Rules, Below Average

16. What do Data Bars do?

Data bars overlay a bar onto a cell based upon its value. The higher the value in the cell relative to the rest of the values in the selected range, the larger the bar.

17. What do Color Scales do?

Color scales overlay a color onto a cell based upon the cell's relative value in relation to the rest of the cells in the selected range. Depending on the option chosen, higher values can be the darkest color in the range or the lightest color in the range. Also, some color scale options use multiple colors so the lowest value might be green while the highest value is red or vice versa.

18. What do Icon Sets do?

Icon sets allow you to display symbols in cells based on their values relative to the other values within the selected range. The symbols you can choose from include colored flags, arrows, or other shapes as well as bars, circles, and stars that are filled in as the value increases relative to the range.

19. Can you customize the limits Excel uses when applying data bars, color scales, and icon sets? How?

Yes. Set up your formatting and then go to Manage Rules under the Conditional Formatting dropdown in the Styles section of the Home tab and choose to Edit the rule. This will bring up a dialogue box where you can then change the criteria to what you want to use.

20. How can you remove conditional formatting from a range of cells?

To remove all formatting from a range of cells, highlight the cells, go to the Style section of the Home tab, click on Conditional Formatting, choose Clear Rules and then choose to clear the rules either from the selected cells or from the entire worksheet.

21. What if you only want to remove one conditional formatting rule from a range of cells, how can you do that?

Select the cells, go the Conditional Formatting dropdown menu, choose Manage Rules, and then delete the rule that you no longer want. You can also just go straight to Manage Rules and edit the range of cells covered by that particular rule.

22. How do you change the order in which conditional formatting rules are applied to a cell or range of cells?

Using the Manage Rules option under the Conditional Formatting dropdown and moving the rules listed for the worksheet into the order you prefer using the up and down arrows.

23. What other option do you have for adding a new conditional formatting rule to your data other than using one of the pre-defined options (Highlight Cells Rules, Top/Bottom Rules, etc.)?

You can also just go to New Rule under the Conditional Formatting dropdown menu. This will bring up the New Formatting Rule dialogue box which will let you specify the type of conditional formatting rule you want to use, the colors, and the values.

INSERTING SYMBOLS
QUIZ ANSWERS

1. How do you insert a symbol into a cell in Excel?

Click into the cell where you want to insert the symbol, go to the Symbols section of the Insert tab, and click on Symbol. This will bring up the Symbol dialogue box. Click on the symbol you want and then click Insert.

2. Can you insert a symbol into a cell that already has text in it?

Yes. Just use the formula bar to click into the location in the existing text for that cell where you want to insert the symbol.

3. Which font has a lot of images like scissors, mailboxes, smiley faces, etc?

Wingdings

4. If you need the copyright symbol or trademark symbol, where can you find those?

The Special Characters tab in the Symbol dialogue box.

5. Can you change the size or color of a symbol you've inserted? If so, how?

Yes. Just highlight it or the cell it's in and then use the options in the Font section of the Home tab.

6. Once you've inserted a symbol into a cell can you change the font without impacting the symbol?

Often times, no. The symbol you've inserted will be tied to the font used and if you change the font the symbol will be replaced by a normal character such as the * sign or [sign. For example, the yin yang sign in Wingdings is actually just the [character in Times New Roman.

PIVOT TABLES
QUIZ ANSWERS

1. What does a pivot table allow you to do?

Take a large amount of data and easily summarize it.

2. How do you need to format your data in order to use a pivot table?

There needs to be a header row that contains labels for each column of data. Below that your data should be arranged in rows with all data for a particular entry contained in that one row. There should be no summary rows or sub-totals in your data. Also remove any blank rows or columns from the data and make sure that you only have one type of data (date, currency, text) in each column.

3. What are some best practices when formatting your data for analysis?

Have a separate column for each data point you might want to analyze. So if you sell blue and green widgets and whatsits, have a column for product color as well as a column for product type. Also try to have standardized values as much as possible. Widgets should always be widgets. Make sure each row of data has all the information you need in it. This may mean repeating information like customer name in multiple rows, but that's okay.

4. How do you start a pivot table?

Highlight your data, go to the Insert tab, and choose Pivot Table from the Tables section.

5. Should you add your pivot table to your existing sheet or to a new one? Why?

Ideally you should add the pivot table to a new worksheet because pivot tables are dynamic and so can expand in terms of number of rows or columns. By adding the pivot table to a new worksheet you ensure that you won't overwrite any existing data.

6. What are the two ways you can add a field to your blank pivot table?

Left-click and drag the field to the spot in the pivot table where you want that field to be. Or left-click and drag the field to the Filters, Rows, Columns, or Values section, whichever you want to use, that's at the bottom of the PivotTable Fields box where it says "Drag fields between areas below."

7. If you drag a field to the Filters section, what can you do with that field?

The field will not appear in the pivot table, but there will be a dropdown menu that allows you to filter the table so that only specified results from that field are included in the table.

8. If you drag a field to the Rows section, how will that field appear in the table?

The values for that field will appear in the table on the left-hand side in rows.

9. If you drag a field to the Columns section, how will that field appear in the table?

The values for that field will appear across the top of the table in columns.

10. If you drag a field to the Values section, how will that field appear in the table?

Excel will calculate a value for that field based upon the intersection of the fields you've placed in the Rows and Columns sections and on any criteria you've filtered by. What value is calculated (sum, count, etc.) will be determined by what you choose.

11. How can you change the function that is performed on a field that you've placed in the Values section?

In the Pivot Table Fields box where you've placed the field, there should be a listing of the field that says something like "Count of [Field Name]" or "Sum of [Field Name]" which tells you what function is currently being performed on that field. Click on the arrow on the right-hand side of the name and choose Value Field Settings. This will bring up the Value Field Settings dialogue box where you can then change the function.

12. What functions can you apply to a field in the Values section?

Sum, Count, Average, Max, Min, Product, Count Numbers, Standard Deviation. You can also choose to show values as a % of the grand total, % of the column total, or % of the row total as well as some other options.

13. If you want to format the values in your table, what are two ways to do so?

You could just highlight the cells and use the formatting options in the Number section of the Home tab. Or you can use the Value Field Settings dialogue box, click on Number Format in the bottom left corner, and format the cells that way.

14. Can you perform two or more calculations on the same field in a pivot table? If so, how?

Yes. You just need to add the field to the Values section for each calculation you want to perform and then change the Value Field Settings to reflect the different calculations you want.

15. Can you have multiple fields for your rows or columns?

Yes.

16. What would be the drawback in doing so?

It can get messy pretty quickly if you have multiple fields in your rows, columns, and values sections.

17. Can you filter which results show for your rows or columns fields? For example, if you just wanted to see one customer's results in the rows section, could you do that? How?

Yes. Use the arrows next to Row Labels and Column Labels to bring up the list of values and uncheck the ones you don't want displayed.

18. Can you reorder the fields in the rows or columns section?

Yes.

19. How can you get the PivotTable tools menu options to display?

Click on your pivot table.

20. What does the Group tool do under Analyze under PivotTable Tools?

It allows you to create an artificial grouping of entries by clicking on each of the items that you want to include in your group.

21. How do you do this?

Hold down the Ctrl key while choosing all the items you want to group together and then choose Group Selection from the Group section of the Analyze tab. You can also choose the items and then right-click and choose Group from the dropdown menu.

22. How do you remove a grouping?

Click on the group name and then choose Ungroup from the Group section of the Analyze tab. You can also right-click and choose Ungroup from the dropdown.

23. If you do have a set of results grouped, how do you see the totals for that group?

Click on the minus sign next to the group name to collapse the entries down to the group level.

24. If you have a set of results grouped and are only able to see the summary for the group, how do you make the individual results visible?

Click on the + sign next to the group name.

25. If you have multiple groups that you want to collapse to the summary level, how can you do this?

Click on Collapse Field in the Active Field section of the Analyze tab.

26. If you have multiple groups that you want to expand at once, how can you do this?

Click on Expand Field in the Active Field section of the Analyze tab.

27. What does the Slicer do?

It works like a filter option, but it's visible to the user.

28. How do you reset any fields you've filtered using the Slicer?

Click on the funnel at the top of the window for the Slicer to clear any filter you have in place.

29. What does Insert Timeline let you do?

Filter the data in your pivot table by month, quarter, year, or day assuming you have a field that Excel recognizes as a date.

30. What does Refresh do?

It allows you to update your pivot table after you've updated your source data.

31. Why is Refresh useful?

Because you may find that your original data has small discrepancies in it, like using Albert Jones and Albert R. Jones, for the same customer and it's much easier to be able to fix those discrepancies and then refresh your table than to rebuild the table from scratch.

32. What issue could you run into using Refresh that you need to be careful about?

Pivot tables are dynamic, meaning they have a variable number of rows and columns in them based upon the data they're displaying. That means each time you refresh a pivot table the number of rows or columns may change and your data may shift. If you've made notes or calculations on the worksheet but outside of the pivot table they may no longer be accurate or they may be erased.

33. What option can you use to change the data that's being used in your pivot table?

Change Data Source.

34. When might you want to change your data in your pivot table?

When you add data for a new month, for example.

35. What should you watch out for when updating your data source?

Sometimes, especially if you try to use the arrow keys, Excel will insert new cell references into the existing cell references, thus ruining the cell range referenced as the data source. It's best, if possible, to just use your cursor to select the range of cells you want.

36. What option can you use to clear your currently selected fields from your pivot table and return to a blank pivot table?

Under the Analyze tab of PivotTable Tools select Clear and then Clear All.

37. What option can you use to just clear any filters you've applied to your pivot table?

Under the Analyze tab of PivotTable Tools select Clear and then Clear Filters.

38. If you want to calculate the value of one field in your table times another field in your table, what's the best way to do this? Where is that option located?

Insert Calculated Field. Located under Fields, Items & Sets.

39. What does the Design tab under PivotTable Tools allow you to do?

Choose how your pivot table displays. It allows you to change the colors, add divider rows, choose when and how to display subtotals, choose when and how to display grand totals, and change the formatting of your row or column headers.

40. Name two ways you can remove a field you've added to a pivot table that you decide you don't want.

Click on the arrow next to the field name in the bottom right corner of the PivotTable Fields table options and choose Remove Field. Or right-click in a cell in the pivot table that contains information from that field and choose "Remove [Field Name]" from the dropdown menu where [Field Name] represents the field you want to remove.

41. How can you change the order of the fields when you have multiple fields for Row, Column, or Value?

Left-click and drag the field to the order you want in the PivotTable Fields table. Or right-click on a cell that contains data for the field you want to move and then go to Move and choose the Move option you want.

42. Can you write formulas that reference cells within a pivot table?

Yes, but it's not easy to do and you can't copy the formulas the same way you would a normal formula because of the way cells in pivot tables are referenced.

43. If you have generated a pivot table and want to use that data elsewhere but don't want to risk having the data update on you, what can you do?

Select All, Copy, and Paste Special – Values. This will convert your pivot table into a simple table of data that can no longer be updated.

44. Is it advisable to create a pivot table and then do calculations on the values of that pivot table outside of the table while leaving it in pivot table format? Why or why not?

No. Because pivot tables are dynamic and can change their rows and columns when updated which can make any external calculations inaccurate or misaligned.

SUBTOTALING AND GROUPING DATA QUIZ ANSWERS

1. What does the Subtotal option let you do?

Take your data and summarize it at each change in a criteria that you specify.

2. Where is the Subtotal option located?

In the Outline section of the Data tab.

3. What must you do before you can subtotal your data?

You must sort your data so that all of the entries you want to subtotal by are grouped together. If you're subtotaling by year, then you want to sort by year. If you're subtotaling by customer, then you want to sort by customer.

4. What will happen if you try to subtotal unsorted data?

Excel will subtotal your data at every change in that criteria. Meaning you might end up with two subtotals for 2013 or three subtotals for Customer Albert Jones, because the entries weren't grouped together, so Excel treated each change as a new grouping.

5. How do you subtotal data?

Select all of the data you want to use, click on Subtotal in the Outline section of the Data tab to bring up the Subtotal dialogue box, and then tell Excel which field to subtotal by, what function to apply when it does so, and which fields to apply that function to.

6. Which field in the Subtotal dialogue box is for the field you want to separate your data by?

The "at each change in" field.

7. Is this the only field Excel will perform the subtotal function on?

No. This is the field that triggers Excel to "subtotal" the data, but it doesn't have to be the field that's subtotaled nor does it have to be the only field that's subtotaled.

8. Can you perform different functions on different fields when you subtotal?

No. You can only perform one function on all of the fields you choose.

9. What functions can you choose to perform using subtotal?

Sum, Count, Average, Max, Min, Product, Count Numbers, StdDev, StdDevp, Var, Varp. (Note that in the guide only the functions up to Product were listed. The rest of these options were pulled by looking in Excel.)

10. How do you choose which fields to apply the function to?

In the Subtotal dialogue box under "add subtotal to" the name of each of the selected fields will be listed. Click in the check box for each field where the function should be applied.

11. Does the field you subtotal by also have to be a field you apply a function to?

No.

12. Can it be?

Yes.

13. What will checking the box for "page break between groups" do?

It will insert a page break at every change in the criteria you chose to subtotal by. So if you chose customer name, then each time there was a change in customer name Excel would "subtotal" the data and insert a page break.

14. What will checking the box for "summary below data" do?

It will insert a Grand Total summary row at the very bottom of your data that shows the calculation of the function you selected for each field you selected for the entire data set.

15. Once you've subtotaled your data, what do the numbers at the left-hand side of the row numbers do?

They allow you to collapse your subtotaled data to the summary level. The 1 will display just the grand total, the 2 will display the subtotals and grand total, and the 3 will display all entries as well as the subtotals and grand total.

16. How do you remove subtotals?

Click on the Subtotal option in the Outline section of the Data tab to bring up the Subtotal dialogue box and choose Remove All.

17. What if you want to keep the subtotals you created, but just remove the grouping options on the left-hand side of the worksheet?

You can either click on Ungroup in the Outline section

of the Data tab and then select Ungroup from the dropdown to remove one group at a time, or you can selected Clear Outline from the dropdown to remove all levels of grouping.

18. What does the Group option allow you to do? Where is it located?

It allows you to group a set of rows or columns so that they can easily be hidden from view and then brought back to view by a simple click on a plus/minus sign. It's located in the Outline section of the Data tab.

19. When might you use this?

When you have data in a table that you don't want to have regularly visible but that you expect you will want to see on occasion. As opposed to Hide Rows or Hide Columns, which are easy to remove but harder to put back in place, using grouping allows you to move back and forth between hidden and visible with ease.

20. How do you group a set of rows or columns?

Select the rows or columns you want to group, choose Group from the Outline section of the Data tab, and then choose Group from the dropdown menu.

21. What is one requirement for any set of rows or columns you want to group?

They must be adjacent to one another. You can't group non-contiguous rows or columns.

22. If you've successfully grouped a set of rows or columns, how will you know?

You'll see a line above the columns or to the left of the rows that has a minus sign at the end. You should also see numbers on the left-hand side of the worksheet showing the grouping levels now available in the worksheet.

23. How can you hide a set of grouped columns or rows?

Click on the minus sign at the end of the line above the columns or to the left of the rows.

24. How can you reveal a set of grouped columns or rows that are currently hidden?

Click on the plus sign above where the columns should be or to the left of where the rows should be.

25. How can you remove all grouping from a worksheet?

Use the Clear Outline option under Ungroup in the Outline section of the Data tab.

26. Should you use Ctrl + Z and Ctrl + Y when using subtotaling or grouping?

Probably not. It's possible that if you have two workbooks open Excel will undo something in your other workbook rather than undo something related to the subtotaling or grouping that you just did. If you do use them, be careful to confirm that whatever you wanted undone was actually undone and not something else.

CHART TYPES
QUIZ ANSWERS

1. What makes charts so useful?

They allow you to visualize your data which will sometimes reveal patterns or insights that aren't readily apparent when just looking at the numbers.

2. How should you configure your data for most charts?

Have a row of labels across the top, another of labels down the side, and record the value for the intersection of those two variables (for example, total sales for that vendor on that date) at the intersection of the two labels in the Excel table.

3. Once you have your data input in Excel, how can you create a chart of it?

Select the data you want to use, go to the Insert tab, and click on the chart type you want to use.

4. How can you preview what your chart will look like?

Instead of clicking on the chart type simply hold your mouse over the chart type you want to use and Excel will display the chart for you. The chart will not be added to your worksheet until you click on it, however.

5. What is time series data?

It's data that shows results over a period of time. So, for example, sales by vendor by month for the year.

6. Which chart options are best for use with time series data?

Column charts, bar charts, and line charts.

7. For data with multiple variables (such as multiple vendors) but no time component (so 2018 summary, for example), what are the best chart options to use?

Pie charts or doughnut charts.

8. What are scatter plots good for?

Random data points where you're looking at the intersection of two or three variables to see if there's a pattern or relationship between the variables.

9. What is the difference between a column chart and a bar chart in Excel?

A column chart has the data displayed in vertical columns. A bar chart has the data displayed in horizontal columns.

10. What does a clustered columns graph do?

The clustered columns graph shows a column for each variable (such as vendor) for each time period (such as month) side-by-side.

11. What are the advantages/disadvantages of a clustered column graph?

You can easily see the difference in results across each variable within a time period, however, if you have a number of variables that you're charting it can quickly become too busy to use.

12. What does the stacked columns graph do?

It displays a single column for each time period that is separated into colored bands where the height of each colored band represents the value for that variable for that time period. It basically takes the columns from the clustered columns graph for each time period and stacks them on top of one another.

13. What are the advantages/disadvantages of a stacked columns graph?

If you have a lot of variables, it's not as busy as the clustered columns graph. It lets you easily see the overall trend across time periods since the height of the column shows overall results for the period. It can sometimes be harder to see changes in individual results for different variables across time.

14. What does the 100% stacked column graph do?

It displays all results for a time period in a single column but instead of the column height being based on values for each variable, it's based on percent share of the whole for the time period. This means that across time periods the height of the column is the same, since the height of the column is always going to be 100%. The colored sections of the column for the time period are the percent that that variable represented of total units for the period.

15. What are the advantages/disadvantages of a 100% stacked column graph?

You can't see any change in value over time. So if you go from earning $10,000 in one period to earning $1,000 in the next but the relative share of earnings for each variable stays the same, you won't see any change in the graph. What it does show nicely is share of return for each variable. So if one variable goes from being 5% of your sales to 50% that will show clearly on a 100% stacked column graph.

16. Is there generally a reason to use 3-D graphs in your presentations?
No.

17. What is a pie chart?
A pie chart is a round chart that shows your results as slices of a pie where the size of each slice is based upon the percent share of the whole for that variable. For example, you might have a pie chart of annual sales at each vendor that shows how much of your revenue came from each one.

18. What is the difference between a pie chart and a doughnut chart?
A doughnut chart is just like a pie chart except it's just the outer edge of the chart and has no center to it.

19. What does a pie of pie chart do?
It takes a pie chart and for the smallest results it creates a second pie chart to display those results in more detail.

20. What does a bar of pie chart do?
It takes a pie chart and for the smallest results it creates a bar chart to display those results in more detail.

21. Which is generally better to use if you must use one, the pie of pie chart or the bar of pie chart?
A bar of pie chart, because there's less likely to be confusion in viewing the results. With a pie of pie chart it's easy to think that the size of the slices in the two pie charts

are comparable, but they are not. The second pie chart is showing % of the small slice it was derived from, not % of the whole.

22. What should you do with your data before using a scatter plot with lines in Excel? Why?

Sort it. Because if you're using a scatter plot that includes lines between points, Excel will draw that line from the first point to the second point, etc. rather than try to draw a smooth line through the data points. If you don't sort your data and try to have Excel draw a line through the points you may get a criss-crossing mess on your graph instead of a smooth path between points.

23. What is the difference between a scatter plot that uses smooth lines and one that uses straight lines?

A smooth line plot will try to create a line that follows a curve between points. A straight line plot will draw a straight line between each point in the graph. Often the difference won't be all that noticeable.

24. What is the difference between a scatter plot with markers and one that doesn't have them?

A scatter plot with markers will place a dot on the graph for every data point. A scatter plot without them will just show the lines that connect the points. This can be an important distinction if you have a data point that's missing.

25. Can you plot more than one set of results on a scatter plot at once? How?

Yes. Just list the results side-by-side with the criteria you want as the horizontal axis listed first. (So Month, Candidate A, Candidate B with the results for each candidate at the intersection of the month's row and the candidate's column.)

EDITING CHARTS QUIZ ANSWERS

1. If the chart you just created has the wrong data points in the wrong places (so maybe it's showing vendor along the axis instead of month), what's one way you can attempt to fix that?

Use the Switch/Row Column option in the Data section of the Design tab under Chart Tools.

2. If you accidentally included a summary row in your chart, how can you easily fix that?

Go to Select Data in the Design tab under Chart Tools to bring up the Select Data Source dialogue box and uncheck the box for that summary row or highlight it and click Remove. You can also double-click on your chart and then go to the data table and click and drag the selected cells boundaries until that row is no longer selected.

3. If you want to add another data point, for example, a new vendor to your existing graph, how can you do that?

Go to Select Data in the Design tab under Chart Tools to bring up the Select Data Source dialogue box and then choose Add, name the series, and select the data you want to include. You can also double-click on the chart and then go to the data table and click and drag the selected cell boundaries until that new data is included.

4. If you want to expand the data points that are included in your chart, how can you do that?

Go to Select Data in the Design tab under Chart Tools to bring up the Select Data Source dialogue box, click on the series you want to edit, choose Edit, and then change the cell references to include the data points you want to include. You can also double-click on the chart and then go to the data table and click and drag the selected cell boundaries to include the new data points.

5. How can you change the order in which the elements in your chart display?

Go to Select Data in the Design tab under Chart Tools to bring up the Select Data Source dialogue box, click on the elements you want to move and use the up and down arrows to move them around.

6. How can you change your chart type?

Click on the chart and then go to the Insert tab and choose your new chart type. Or go to the Design tab under Chart Tools, choose Change Chart Type, and choose your chart type from there.

7. What are Chart Styles?

Pre-formatted templates for each chart type that include a variety of color options and various chart elements. They can be a quick way to format a chart if the elements and colors work for what you need.

8. How can you apply a Chart Style to a chart?

Click on the chart, go to the Design tab under Chart Tools, and look at the available options in the Chart Styles section of the tab. Click on the one you want.

9. Do you have to select a Chart Style to see what it will look like with your data?

No. You can just hold your mouse over the style and Excel will show you what the chart will look like using that style. It will not, however, permanently apply the style until you click on it.

10. Does a Chart Style have to be exactly what you want for you to use it?

No. You can start by applying a chart style and then customize it from there.

11. What is a Quick Layout?

The Quick Layout option is another option you have for formatting a chart that provides a variety of layout options to choose from that mostly involve different configurations of the axis labels, chart title, legend, etc. It will not change any of your chart colors like Chart Styles will.

12. How can you apply a Quick Layout to your chart?

Click on the chart and then go to the Design tab under Chart Tools and in the Chart Layouts section click on the Quick Layout dropdown and choose the layout you want.

13. Do you have to click on a Quick Layout option to see what it will look like on your chart?

No. You can hold your cursor over each option to see what it will look like before you actually apply it to your chart.

14. Can you further customize a chart after you've applied a Quick Layout to it?

Yes.

15. Can you use both a Chart Style and Quick Layout on the same chart? If so, what challenges are there to doing so?

Yes, but only if you do it in the right order. If you

choose Chart Style first and then use a Quick Layout you'll keep the color scheme and background colors from the Chart Style but the positioning of the chart elements from the Quick Layout. If you use the Quick Layout first, the Chart Style will overwrite the Quick Layout when you apply it.

16. What's the easiest way to change the colors in your chart?

Use Change Colors which provides you with pre-defined color palettes to choose from and is available in the Design tab under Chart Tools. (You can also use Shape Styles under the Format tab under Chart Tools to change the color of specific elements in your chart one at a time using pre-defined options.)

17. What chart elements can you add or delete from a chart?

Axes, Axis Titles, Chart Title, Data Labels, Data Table, Error Bars, Gridlines, Legend, Lines, Trendline, and Up/Down Bars

18. Where can you go under Chart Tools to add chart elements to your chart?

Under Add Chart Elements in the Chart Layouts section of the Design tab.

19. What does the Axes option allow you to do?

Add or delete data point labels to each axis of your chart. (So along the bottom or side of the chart.)

20. What does the Axis Titles option allow you to do?

Add a title to each axis of your chart. If there already is a title for an axis, you can also remove it.

21. When you use Axis Titles, is the title for that axis already populated?

No. It says "Axis Title". You'll need to click into the title box and replace that with the label you want.

22. What does Chart Title allow you to do?

Allows you to either remove the existing chart title or change where the title is located on the chart (at the top or overlaid on the chart itself).

23. What does Data Labels allow you to do?

Label each of the data points in your chart with its value.

24. When can Data Labels be particularly useful?

With pie charts where there aren't axes to show the values.

25. What does Data Table allow you to do?

Add or remove a table underneath your chart that shows the data that was used to create the chart. It can either include legend keys that let you tie the entries in the table to the chart using color-matching or not.

26. What does Gridlines let you do?

Add (or remove) horizontal or vertical lines to your chart which can make it easier to identify the approximate values represented in your chart.

27. What does Legend do?

Let you determine the location of the chart's legend, which is the color-coded guide that tells you what color represents what data point. It can be at the top, bottom, left, or right-hand side. You can also remove it entirely, but that's not recommended unless you're using a Data Table with Legend Keys.

28. What does Trendline allow you to do?

Add a line onto your line chart that shows the overall

trend in the data for that variable. (So, for a specific vendor, for example.)

29. How can you change the size of your chart?

Click on the chart and then left-click and drag on one of the white boxes along the perimeter of the chart. You can also click on the chart to pull up the Format Chart Area formatting task pane and then go to the Size & Properties option and input a size there.

30. How can you move a chart to a new position within your worksheet?

Left-click on an empty space within the chart, hold that left-click, and drag the chart to where you want it. (If you click on a chart element, you may end up moving the chart element instead of the chart.)

31. How can you move a chart to a new worksheet or other document?

Click on an empty space within the chart and then use Ctrl + C to copy the chart or Ctrl + V to cut it from its current location, go to where you want to place the chart, and use Ctrl + V to paste it there. (You can also use the other cut/copy/paste options like right-clicking and selecting from the dropdown or going to the Clipboard section of the Home tab. The control shortcuts are just the quickest way to do it.)

32. How can you manually rearrange the elements within a chart, such as the chart title?

Left-click on the element you want to move, hold that down, and drag it to where you want it.

33. Can you move all elements in a chart?

No. Not all of the elements will move.

34. How do you change the title of a chart?

Left-click on the chart title, click into the box to highlight the existing text, delete it, and add your own text.

35. How do you change the name of a data field that's displayed in the legend of your chart?

Your best approach is to do so in the original data table. When you do that the legend will update. (You could also go to the Select Data option in the Design tab under Chart Tools to bring up the Select Data Source dialogue box and then choose to Edit that element and change the Series name from a cell reference to text. If you do that, however, that creates a disconnect between your data table and your chart that you need to remember exists.)

36. How can you apply custom colors to your chart elements?

Use the Format Tab under Chart Tools to apply colors to each chart element separately. To do so, click on the element you want to change, go to the Format tab under Chart Tools, and click on Shape Fill or Shape Outline and then choose your color.

37. When should you use Shape Fill?

To change the color of the elements in bar, column, or pie charts. Or the interior of 3-D chart elements.

38. When should you use Shape Outline?

To change the color of the elements in a line graph or for the border of 3-D chart elements.

39. What do you need to be careful of when applying custom colors to your chart?

That you've only selected the portion of the chart that applies to one data element at a time. It's very easy to accidentally change the color of all chart elements at once, especially with pie charts.

40. If you mess up, what's the easiest way to fix it?
Ctrl + Z to undo and then try again.

41. What does the Formatting Task Pane do?
Gives you another way to edit your chart that sometimes has more options than the menu options available under Chart Tools.

42. If you want to have the segments in your pie chart separated to make them more clearly visible, where can you go to do this?
The Pie Explosion option under Series Options in the Format Data Series formatting task pane.

43. Can you use the Home tab Font options to edit the font color, size, or style in a chart?
Yes.

REMOVING DUPLICATE ENTRIES
QUIZ ANSWERS

1. If you have a column that has duplicate values and you want to narrow the list down to just unique values, how can you do that?

Use Remove Duplicates which is located in the Data Tools section of the Data tab.

2. In the Remove Duplicates dialogue box, what does checking the "my data has headers" box do?

It excludes the first row of your data from the analysis. If you don't check that box the first row will be treated just like any other row in your data.

3. When you have Excel remove duplicates from a single column of data what happens to that data?

You're left with one unique occurrence of each value and the data is consolidated into continuous rows. So if you had 100 entries in that column and there were ten unique values spread across the hundred rows, those ten values will now show as the first ten entries in the column no matter where they were located in the column before that.

4. Can you remove duplicate values across multiple columns?

Yes.

5. How does that work?

If you choose to remove duplicate values across Columns A and B then Excel will evaluate the combination of the values in Column A and B for each row to determine if duplicates exist. In that case, for example, you might end up with ABC Corp, Nevada and ABC Corp, New York as separate entries because they're unique combinations of the values in Columns A and B.

6. Can you remove duplicates from two out of six columns in a data range? Should you?

You can but you shouldn't. If you just select the two columns and remove duplicates Excel will consolidate those entries in those two columns so that they're no longer aligned with the data in the other four columns. If you select all six and choose to remove duplicates from two of the six, when Excel removes duplicates it will delete the data for the other four columns where duplicates existed. You'll end up losing data and having no real way to see that that happened.

7. Why should you always do any calculations or manipulations on a copy of your source data instead of the original copy?

Because there are some errors you cannot fix and will not know you have made until it's too late to undo them. By keeping a clean copy of your original data this allows you to always go back and start over from scratch. If you don't keep a clean copy of your original data you may do something to your data (like remove duplicates improperly) that you can't fix.

CONVERTING TEXT TO COLUMNS
QUIZ ANSWERS

1. What does Text to Columns allow you to do?

It allows you to take information that's all in one cell and split it out across multiple columns based upon the criteria you specify.

2. What is the most basic use of Text to Columns?

When dealing with a .csv file that has one long entry per row where each column's data is indicated by a comma. (Although more recent versions of Excel do this conversion for you automatically.)

3. Before you apply Text to Columns to a column of data what should you do?

Check to make sure that there is no information in the columns to the right of that column that will be overwritten when you apply Text to Columns.

4. If I have a list of entries in Column A that are first name space last name, so "Mark Jones", "Dave Clark", etc. how can I separate that list into two

columns, one with first name and one with last name and with no extra spaces?

Click on Column A, go to the Data Tools section of the Data tab and select Text to Columns. In the Convert Text to Columns Wizard dialogue box choose the Delimited option and then click Next. On the second screen choose Space and check the box so that consecutive delimiters are treated as one. Click Finish.

5. If I have a list of entries in Column A where each entry starts with a two-digit number that indicates the year and is followed by a five-digit customer ID, how can I separate the two-digit year into one column and the five-digit ID into another column?

Click on Column A, go to the Data Tools section of the Data tab and select Text to Columns. In the Convert Text to Columns Wizard dialogue box choose the Fixed Width option and then click Next. On the second screen click onto the data preview to put a break line after the first two digits in the number. Click Finish.

6. When you use the Delimiter option, what happens to your delimiter?

It's deleted.

7. How can you delete a break line you placed that you don't want to use?

Double-click on it.

8. How can you move a break line you placed that isn't in the right location?

Click on it and drag it to where you want it to go.

9. Can you choose more than one delimiter (say a space and a comma) under the Delimiter option?

Yes.

10. Can you specify a custom delimiter? How?

Yes. Check the Other box and then type in the delimiter you want to use.

11. Can you specify how you're newly-separated data will be formatted? How?

Yes. On the final screen of the Convert Text to Columns Wizard.

12. What do you need to be careful of when using the Delimiter option with Convert Text to Columns?

Not all data entries are the same dimensions and so using a delimiter may end up with one entry being split into three columns while another is split into two columns. This is especially true when working with a data set that wasn't built to be split. For example, if you have an employee "Mark Jones" and another who is "David Allen Marks" and you split those names using a space delimiter you will have Mark and Jones in two columns but then you will have David, Allen, and Marks in three columns and the middle name of David Allen Marks will be lined up with the last name of Mark Jones.

13. What function allows you to remove excess spaces from around text?

TRIM

CONCATENATE QUIZ ANSWERS

1. What does the CONCATENATE function let you do?

According to Excel it allows you to join several text strings into one. The strings of information you can combine include numbers, symbols, punctuation, and values in other cells.

2. What is the basic format of a CONCATENATE function?

=CONCATENATE(text1, [text2],...) where each element in the function is separated by a comma and each "text" entry can either be a cell reference or a text entry indicated by quotation marks at the beginning and the end of the text.

3. Let's say you have customer first name in Cell A1, customer last name in Cell B1, and that you want to create an entry that's "LastName, FirstName" (last name comma space first name) using those values. How would you write that using the CONCATENATE function?

=CONCATENATE(B1,", ",A1)

4. How would you create an entry that's "FirstName Last Name" (first name space last name)?

=CONCATENATE(A1," ",B1)

5. What would the result be from the function =CONCATENATE("Jones",", ","Albert")? What does the ", " portion in the center represent? And why do we need the quotation marks around Jones and Albert?

You would get:

Jones, Albert

The ", " portion adds a comma followed by a space in the middle of the two text entries. It's in quotation marks because it's referring to text. That's why there are quotation marks around Jones and Albert as well since they're text entries not cell references. A cell reference does not require quotation marks but text does.

6. After you've used the CONCATENATE function to create an entry, what do you need to be careful about with respect to the entry you've created?

It's still a function, which means that even though it looks like a text entry it's using other cells to create the entry. If you delete the other cells that are feeding into the function it will impact your CONCATENATE function as well and change what's displayed.

7. How can you address this issue?

Once your CONCATENATE entry looks the way you want it to, copy it and then Paste Special – Values so that the formula is removed and just the text remains.

THE IF FUNCTION QUIZ ANSWERS

1. What does an IF function do?

It allows you to return different results depending on whether the criteria you specify are met or not.

2. Translate the IF function =IF(A2>25,0,A2*0.05) into a written description.

IF Cell A2 has a value greater than 25 then return a value of zero. Otherwise, return a value equal to the value in Cell A2 times .05.

3. What is another way to think about the components of an IF function?

IF(If, Then, Else) or IF A, THEN B, ELSE C or IF A, THEN B, OTHERWISE C.

4. What does it mean that you can nest IF functions?

It means that you can start with one IF function and then replace either the THEN component or the ELSE component with another IF function so that you get IF A, THEN B, ELSE, IF C, THEN D, OTHERWISE E, for example.

5. If you're going to nest IF functions, which is it better to replace, the Then portion or the Else portion? Why?

The Else portion. Because then that keeps all of the parts of each individual IF function together as opposed to splitting them up across the function.

6. Translate the IF function =IF(A9>A5,B5, IF(A9>A4,B4,0)) into a written description.

If the value in Cell A9 is greater than the value in Cell A5, then return the value in Cell B5. Otherwise, if the value in Cell A9 is greater than the value in Cell A4, return the value in Cell B4. Otherwise return a value of zero.

7. If you were to copy the above formula into a new cell, how would it change?

The only thing that would change is the cell reference to cell A9, the rest of the function uses $ signs to refer to specified cells. It's using a table to generate the results of the IF function.

8. If you have a long and complex nested IF function that you can't get to work, what are some ways you can troubleshoot the IF function to figure out what's wrong?

Arrow through the function to make sure that you have the correct number of opening and closing parens. For each IF in the function there should be one opening paren immediately after the IF and a corresponding closing paren somewhere in the funtion.

Replace all but one of the IF functions with a placeholder result to create a simple IF function and evaluate whether it's doing what it should. So, for example, =IF(A9>A5,B5,IF(A9>A4,B4,0)) would become =IF(A9>A5,B5,"ELSE") where the second IF function has temporarily been replaced with a result of ELSE.

9. What is the most likely issue if Excel tells you you've entered too many arguments with an IF function?

You probably have a misplaced paren somewhere. (Older versions of Excel did limit the number of IF functions you could nest, but in current versions you're unlikely to have too many IF functions nested.)

10. What should you always do with an IF function that you create? (Or any function really?)

Test it to make sure it's doing what it should be. Pay particular attention to threshold results where the result should transition from one result to another. For example, did you mean greater than or did you mean greater than or equal to and how did you actually write it?

11. If you write an IF function that's referencing a table of fixed values (like a discount table) what should you always be sure to do?

Use $ signs when writing the references to those cells so that you can easily copy your IF function while keeping the table references fixed.

COUNTIFS QUIZ ANSWERS

1. What does the COUNTIFS function do?

It allows you to count how many times a set of criteria are met with a data set. So, for example, how many customers are from Alaska and buy Whatsits.

2. How does this differ from the COUNTIF function?

The COUNTIF function does the same thing but for only one criteria.

3. Which should you use?

If you have Excel 2007 or later, you should use COUNTIFS instead of COUNTIF because you can replicate the results of COUNTIF using COUNTIFS. Prior to Excel 2007 COUNTIFS did not exist so you'll be stuck with COUNTIF and unable to do the more complex counts available through using COUNTIFS.

4. What is the following function doing:
=COUNTIFS(B2:B6,"Alaska")

It is saying to count the number of entries in Cells B2 through B6 that have the text value Alaska.

5. What is the following function doing:
=COUNTIFS(A1:A10,">25")

It is saying to count the number of entries in Cells A1 through A10 where the value is greater than 25.

6. What is the following function doing:
=COUNTIFS(C10:C200,"*a*")

It is saying to count the number of entries in Cells C10 through C200 where the entry includes the letter a anywhere in the cell.

7. What is the following function doing:
=COUNTIFS(C10:C200,"*e")

It is saying to count the number of entries in Cells C10 through C200 where the entry includes the letter e at the end of a word.

8. Could any of the above four examples also be written using the COUNTIF function?

Yes. Since they only have one count criteria, they could work equally well with COUNTIF.

9. What is the following function doing: =COUNTIFS (C10:C200,"Alaska",D10:D200,"Whatsits")

It is saying to count the number of entries in Rows 10 through 200 where the value in Column C is Alaska and the value in Column D is Whatsits.

10. Could you use COUNTIF with the above example?

No, because there are two count criteria.

11. What do you need to watch out for in terms of your cell ranges when using multiple count criteria?

That the cell ranges for each of your count criteria are the same dimensions. So the same number of rows down and/or columns across so that Excel can match the entries across your count criteria.

12. Can you have a COUNTIFS function that includes a text criteria and a numeric criteria both?

Yes.

13. If you write a COUNTIFS function that references the values in three separate columns, say Columns A, B, and C, how will Excel look at the data to make its count. For example, with the formula =COUNTIFS (A:A,"Alaska",B:B,"Whatsits",C:C,"Paid") what is Excel going to look at to make its count?

It's going to look at each Row to see if the values in each of those columns are Alaska, Whatsits, and Paid. Only if the columns in a row contain those results will Excel count the entry.

14. If you write a COUNTIFS function that references the values in three separate rows, say Rows 1, 2 and 3, how will Excel look at the data to make its count. For example, with the formula =COUNTIFS (1:1,"Alaska",2:2,"Whatsits",3:3,"Paid") what is Excel going to look at to make its count?

It's going to look at each Column to see if the values in each of those rows are Alaska, Whatsits, and Paid. Only if the rows in a column contain those results will Excel count the entry.

15. What is one thing you can do when setting up a COUNTIFS function to make sure it's working before you expand it to your entire worksheet?

Start with a smaller sample that only has a few variables that you can test for issues in your formula. But also be sure that you've tested all possible scenarios. So if your criteria is "*e" then make sure you've tested words that start with e, have an e in the middle, and end with e to see if the count you get is what you expected.

SUMIFS QUIZ ANSWERS

1. What does the SUMIFS function do?

It allows you to sum a value that you specify based upon whether one or more other criteria are met.

2. How does it differ from the SUMIF function?

SUMIFS allows you specify multiple criteria that must be met before a value is summed. SUMIF only allows you to specify one variable.

3. When was it introduced?

Excel 2007, so those who have older versions of Excel don't have access to SUMIFS, they only have access to SUMIF.

4. If you start by writing a SUMIF function and realize you want to write a SUMIFS function, can you do that?

No. The order of the arguments are different in a SUMIFS function than they are in a SUMIF function so you would have to start over.

5. If you have access to both SUMIF and SUMIFS, which should you use?

SUMIFS. Because SUMIF and SUMIFS order their variables differently it's a best practice to always use SUMIFS even if you have just one sum criteria.

6. Write a description of what =SUMIFS(A1:A10, B1:B10, "NZD",C1:C10,"") is saying?

To sum the values in each row in Column A when the value in Column B for that row is NZD and the cell in Column C for that row is blank.

7. How would you write a SUMIFS function to sum the values in Column C when the values in Column D are greater than 30 and the value in Column E is Smith?

=SUMIFS(C:C,D:D,">30",E:E,"Smith")

8. Can you apply SUMIFS to a range of cells (so two columns and two rows) and not just a column or row?

Yes.

9. If you can, what do you need to make sure of?

That the dimensions of all of your ranges are the same. So if your sum group is 2x2 then your criteria groups must also be 2x2.

TEXT FUNCTION QUIZ ANSWERS

1. What does the TEXT function do?

According to Excel the TEXT function "converts a value to text in a specific format" but it's also a way to convert date entries to their day of the week or month of the year equivalents and to format a number.

2. If the value in Cell A1 is 5 and you use =TEXT(A1, "$0.00") what result will you get?

$5.00

3. If the value in Cell A1 is 5 and you use =TEXT(A1, "#.00") what result will you get?

5.00

4. If the value in Cell A1 is 5 and you use =TEXT(A1, "#.#0") what result will you get?

5.0

5. If the value in Cell A1 is 5 and you use =TEXT(A1, "#.##") what result will you get?

5.

6. If the value in Cell A1 is 4.235 and you use =TEXT (A1,"$0.00") what result will you get?

$4.24

7. If the value in Cell A1 is 4.235 and you use =TEXT (A1,"#.00") what result will you get?

4.24

8. If the value in Cell A1 is 4.235 and you use =TEXT (A1,"#.#0") what result will you get?

4.24

9. If the value in Cell A1 is 4.235 and you use =TEXT (A1,"#.##") what result will you get?

4.24

10. What is the difference between using a 0 and a # sign in the above examples?

A zero will force a specified number of decimal places to show even if they're not needed. This is why the examples with .00 and the value of 5 return 5.00 as a result. A pound sign will display up to that number of decimal places but won't force them if they're not needed. That's why the example with the #.## and the 5 doesn't have any numbers showing after the decimal.

11. What do you need to watch for when using the # sign for formatting?

That you don't create a situation like the example above where the number becomes 5. with the decimal but without any numbers after the decimal. It's better if you want a number to use a decimal place that at least one of the formatting symbols you put after the decimal is a zero instead of a pound sign.

12. If the value in Cell A1 is 4.235 and you use =TEXT(A1,"$#.##") & " per unit" what result will

you get?
$4.24 per unit

13. How can you take a date from Cell A1 and display its day of the week written fully? For example, Sunday.
=TEXT(A1,"dddd")

14. How can you display its abbreviated day of the week? For example, Sun.
=TEXT(A1,"ddd")

15. How can you isolate what day of the month it is from a date in Cell A1?
=TEXT(A1,"dd") or =TEXT(A1,"d") depending on whether you want a single-digit number or a two-digit number for the first days of the month.

16. How can you take a date from Cell A1 and display its month of the year written fully? For example, November.
=TEXT(A1,"mmmm")

17. How can you display its abbreviated month of the year? For example, Nov.
=TEXT(A1,"mmm")

18. How can you isolate the number for the month of the year from a date in Cell A1?
=TEXT(A1,"mm") or =TEXT(A1,"m") depending on whether you want a single-digit number or a two-digit number for the first months of the year.

19. How can you isolate the year from a date in Cell A1?
=TEXT(A1,"yy") or =TEXT(A1,"yyyy") depending on whether you want a two-digit or a four-digit year.

LIMITING ALLOWED INPUTS QUIZ ANSWERS

1. What is the issue that you run into if you let users enter data in any way they choose?

You can't easily analyze your data because of all of the variations in how people input the same information. One user might use USA, another might use U.S.A., another might use United States, and another might use U.S.. When you try to analyze data like that Excel (and most databases) will treat each of those values separately. It won't know that they all mean the same thing.

2. How can you get around this issue?

By limiting the answers that your users can provide. If you, for example, provide a dropdown list for users to choose from when entering Country, then you guarantee that only one value will be used for each country and that that data will be standardized.

3. What issue can you run into if you provide a dropdown menu of choices?

If you don't think through possible answers, you can

end up with a situation where users aren't able to provide the response they need to. For example, if you had a list of countries and you left Australia off the list and then had a customer from Australia, your users wouldn't be able to correctly list the customer's country.

4. What's one way around this?

Provide an Other category that includes a free-text option to capture those situations where your list of available inputs was missing a needed value and then monitor that list to add new values as needed to the main list.

5. What's one danger of doing this?

Users will use the Other category when they shouldn't and you are once more faced with data that should be grouped together that isn't because of poor data input.

6. How can you limit the values someone can input into a cell in Excel (general)?

Highlight the cells where you want to limit the input, click on Data Validation in the Data Tools section of the Data tab and then click on Data Validation again to bring up the Data Validation dialogue box and specify the limits you want.

7. If you want to limit users to a list of accepted text entries, what option should you choose? How do you specify the list?

Select the List option under Allow and then click into the Source box and highlight your list of accepted values. (It's best to have this be a list within the Excel worksheet, preferably on another worksheet that you then hide from users so that it's always available but can't be edited.)

8. If you want to limit users to only entering whole numbers, what option should you choose?

Whole Number.

9. If you want users to be able to enter a decimal number instead, what option should you choose?

Decimal.

10. When limiting a user's input to a number (either whole or decimal), what else do you need to do? And what should you be careful about when doing so?

Specify an accepted range of values that the user can enter. Think through possible values a user might need to enter. If you, for example, don't allow negative values or don't allow large enough values, this could restrict your users unnecessarily.

11. What will happen if you've applied data validation to a cell and a user tries to input an answer that isn't allowed?

Excel will generate an error message telling them that their entry isn't allowed.

12. Can you customize the message that displays? Where?

Yes. Under Error Alert.

13. How can you remove data validation from a set of cells?

Highlight the cells where you want to remove the data validation, go to the Data Tools section of the Data tab and click on Data Validation and then select Data Validation to bring up the Data Validation dialogue box, and choose Clear All in the bottom left corner.

LOCKING CELLS OR WORKSHEETS
QUIZ ANSWERS

1. Is it possible to keep users from editing the contents of cells in a worksheet? If so, how?

Yes. Select the range of cells that you want to lock from editing, right-click, choose Format Cells, and in the Format Cells dialogue box go to the Protection tab and choose Locked. Click OK. Next, go to the Cells section of the Home tab and click on Format and choose Protect Sheet from the dropdown menu. Provide a password to lock the worksheet and specify what users are allowed to do with locked cells.

You can also add protection to a worksheet or entire workbook using Protect Sheet or Protect Workbook under the Changes section of the Review tab.

2. What do you need to watch out for when locking a worksheet?

First, that you remember the password you used. Second, that you don't lock down so much that users can't use the worksheet. For example, if you lock column width and the values returned are large enough that the data displays as ####, that's not helpful to your users.

3. How can you remove protection from a worksheet?

Go back to the Format dropdown in the Cells section of the Home tab and choose Unprotect Sheet and provide your password. You can also remove protection from a worksheet or entire workbook using Protect Sheet or Protect Workbook under the Changes section of the Review tab.

4. Is it possible to hide the contents of cells in a worksheet as well? How?

Yes. Just click the Hidden box as well as the Locked box when you're protecting your cells.

HIDING A WORKSHEET
QUIZ ANSWERS

1. How can you hide a worksheet?

Right-click on the worksheet name and select Hide.

2. How can you unhide a worksheet?

Right-click on the name of any visible worksheet and choose Unhide. From there select from the dialogue box which worksheet(s) you want to unhide.

3. How can you hide a worksheet and keep someone from unhiding it?

Hide the worksheet and also protect the workbook. If the workbook has been locked then no one will be able to unhide the worksheet unless they have the password to remove protection from the workbook first.

TWO-VARIABLE ANALYSIS
GRID QUIZ ANSWERS

1. What does a two-variable analysis grid let you do?

It lets you create a table where you calculate possible outcomes given the values of two different variables. For example, hourly wage and hours worked to calculate amount earned for a week.

2. What shortcut can you use to make it easy to create a two-variable analysis grid?

Use the $ sign to fix your column and row references so that you only have to write the formula once and can then just copy and paste it to the rest of the table.

3. How can you combine a two-variable analysis grid with conditional formatting?

You can build the grid and then use conditional formatting to flag the results that meet your criteria. So, for example, if you need to earn $1,000 per week you can build a table with hourly wage and hours worked and then use conditional formatting to highlight in green all combinations where the amount earned is $1,000 or more.

MORE ANSWERS
QUIZ ANSWERS

1. What are three ways that you can find out more information on a topic from within Excel?

Hold your cursor over items in the menu section to see a description of what they do. Click on the Tell Me More option that's available under some of the menu items in Excel, such as Format Painter. Click on the question mark in the top right corner and search by subject.

2. What's the best way to find a function or learn more about a function you want to use?

Go to Insert Function under the Formulas tab and bring up the Insert Function dialogue box. Type in the function name that interests you or search by what you want to do. Once you have the function listed in the Select a Function box, click on it to see a brief description and format. If that's not enough, click on the Help on This Function link at the bottom of the dialogue box. You can also double-click on the function name to bring up the Function Arguments dialogue box which will give you a sample output and show how to build the function.

3. If you need more information than that, what options do you have outside of Excel?

Do an internet search and click on the support.office.com option. Look for user forums where your issue has already been discussed. Email me.

4. When is it better to use a forum than go to the Microsoft website?

When you need to know if it's possible to do something in Excel or want to know how to use a function for a specific purpose. The Microsoft website is good for functional questions but not is it possible type questions.

5. What's a nice trick you can use when troubleshooting a function?

Double-click on the cell that has the function in it and Excel will color-code the cell references in the formula as well as the actual cells being referred to by each cell reference. This can be a quick way to see that the wrong range of cells are being referenced by the formula or that ones that should be included aren't.

6. If you do something you didn't want to do, what's the easiest way to reverse it?

Ctrl + Z, Undo.

7. What's a best practice if you're building a really complex worksheet or one with lots of moving parts?

Save versions of the document so that if you do make a mistake you can't take back you don't lose all of your work. So solve one issue, save a copy, solve the next one, save a new copy, etc.

8. If you're using dates in your files names why use the YYYYMMDD format to record the date?

Because when you sort your file names, they'll sort in chronological order.

BONUS: EXERCISES

EXERCISE 1

Create a two-variable analysis grid that looks at home sale prices from $325,000 to $400,000 in increments of $25,000 and sales costs of 3%, 4%, 5%, and 6% with a mortgage balance due of $300,000.

Calculate what someone would net if they sold their property at each of those prices and sales costs given that mortgage balance? Apply conditional formatting so that all outcomes with a net of $32,500 or more are colored green.

EXERCISE 2

Starting with a grid like this one

	A	B	C	D	E	F
1	Sample A	Sample B	Sample C	Sample D	Sample E	Sample F
2	1	1	1	1	1	1
3	2	2	2	2	2	2
4	3	3	3	3	3	3
5	4	4	4	4	4	4
6	5	5	5	5	5	5
7	6	6	6	6	6	6
8	7	7	7	7	7	7
9	8	8	8	8	8	8
10	9	9	9	9	9	9
11	10	10	10	10	10	10

create the following conditional formats in Columns B through F:

Sample B: No values visible but each cell is marked with either an ex, an exclamation point, or a check mark based upon its position within the range of values from 1 through

10. The first three with an ex, the next four with an exclamation mark, and the final three with a checkmark.

Sample C: The text for any cell that has a value between 5 and 7 is colored blue and bolded.

Sample D: Cells are filled with a solid bar of color that is bigger the larger the value, but all values below 2 are grouped together in the lowest range and all values 8 and up are grouped together in the highest range.

Sample E: Apply shaded color to the cells with the darkest color for the highest value. Customize the color to shade from light gold to dark gold.

Sample F: Apply a purple fill color and white font to the top 20% of the values in the range.

EXERCISE 3

Recreate the following table (formatting optional) and then provide answers to the questions below :

	A	B	C	D
1	Customer	Date	Units	Product
2	Jones	1/1/2018	5	Whatsit
3	Smith	1/2/2018	10	Whatsit
4	Baker	1/3/2018	25	Whatsit
5	Smith	1/4/2018	25	Thingy
6	Baker	1/5/2018	10	Thingy
7	Jones	1/6/2018	5	Thingy
8	Baker	1/7/2018	5	Whatsit
9	Jones	1/8/2018	5	Whatsit
10	Jones	1/9/2018	10	Whatsit
11				

1. How many total units has Customer Jones purchased?

2. How many Whatsits has Customer Baker purchased?

3. How many Thingies did Customer Smith purchase?

4. How many total units were purchased between January 1st and January 4th?

EXERCISE 4

Using the below data, create a stacked bar chart, a clustered column chart, and a line chart for the monthly entries and a pie chart using the YTD column.

For the line chart include a data table with legend keys and remove the legend.

For the bar chart change the default colors.

For the pie chart add labels that show the total value for each slice on the outside and explode the pie so that the slices are slightly separated.

	A	B	C	D	E	F	G	H
1		January	February	March	April	May	June	YTD
2	Alpha	15	20	25	30	35	40	165
3	Beta	25	23	21	19	17	15	120
4	Omega	10	20	10	20	10	20	90

EXERCISE 5

Using the same data from Exercise 3, isolate a list of your unique customer names and write a function that will sum the total number of units each customer bought. Assume your data covers thousands of rows and that you may be dealing with hundreds of customer names.

	A	B	C	D
1	**Customer**	**Date**	**Units**	**Product**
2	Jones	1/1/2018	5	Whatsit
3	Smith	1/2/2018	10	Whatsit
4	Baker	1/3/2018	25	Whatsit
5	Smith	1/4/2018	25	Thingy
6	Baker	1/5/2018	10	Thingy
7	Jones	1/6/2018	5	Thingy
8	Baker	1/7/2018	5	Whatsit
9	Jones	1/8/2018	5	Whatsit
10	Jones	1/9/2018	10	Whatsit
11				

BONUS:
EXERCISE ANSWERS

EXERCISE 1

Create a two-variable analysis grid that looks at home sale prices from $325,000 to $400,000 in increments of $25,000 and sales costs of 3%, 4%, 5%, and 6% with a mortgage balance due of $300,000.

Calculate what someone would net if they sold their property at each of those prices and sales costs given that mortgage balance? Apply conditional formatting so that all outcomes with a net of $32,500 or more are colored green.

* * *

There are multiple ways to create the above, but here is one way:

	A	B	C	D	E	F
1	Mortgage	$300,000				
2						
3				Sales Price		
4			$325,000	$350,000	$375,000	$400,000
5	Sale Cost	3%	$15,250	$39,500	$63,750	$88,000
6		4%	$12,000	$36,000	$60,000	$84,000
7		5%	$8,750	$32,500	$56,250	$80,000
8		6%	$5,500	$29,000	$52,500	$76,000

1. In Cell A1 type "Mortgage".

2. In Cell B1 type "$300,000".

3. In Cell C3 type "Sales Price".

4. In Cell C4 type "$325,000". In Cell D4 use the formula =C4+25000. Copy the formula from Cell D4 to Cells E4 through F4. Add a border and fill color to Cells C4 through F4.

5. Select Cells C3 through F3 and Merge & Center. Add a basic border and fill color to the newly created cell.

6. In Cell B5 type "3%". In Cell B6 use the formula =B5+.01. Copy the formula from Cell B6 to Cells B7 and B8. Add a border and fill color to Cells B5 through B8.

7. In Cell A5 type "Sale Cost".

8. Select Cells A5 through A8 and Merge & Center. Change the text orientation in the cell to Rotate Text Up. Add a border and fill color to the newly created cell. Middle Align the cell.

9. In Cell C5 add the formula =(C$4*(1-$B5))-B1. Copy the formula from Cell C5 to Cells C5 through F8. Add a border to Cells C5 through F8.

10. Select Cells C5 through F8 and apply Greater Than conditional formatting to the cells to color those with a value equal to or greater than $32,500 green.

EXERCISE 2

Starting with a grid like this one

	A	B	C	D	E	F
1	Sample A	Sample B	Sample C	Sample D	Sample E	Sample F
2	1	1	1	1	1	1
3	2	2	2	2	2	2
4	3	3	3	3	3	3
5	4	4	4	4	4	4
6	5	5	5	5	5	5
7	6	6	6	6	6	6
8	7	7	7	7	7	7
9	8	8	8	8	8	8
10	9	9	9	9	9	9
11	10	10	10	10	10	10

create the following conditional formats in Columns B through F:

Sample B: No values visible but each cell is marked with either an ex, an exclamation point, or a check mark based upon its position within the range of values from 1 through

10. The first three with an ex, the next four with an exclamation mark, and the final three with a checkmark.

Sample C: The text for any cell that has a value between 5 and 7 is colored blue and bolded.

Sample D: Cells are filled with a solid bar of color that is bigger the larger the value, but all values below 2 are grouped together in the lowest range and all values 8 and up are grouped together in the highest range.

Sample E: Apply shaded color to the cells with the darkest color for the highest value. Customize the color to shade from light gold to dark gold.

Sample F: Apply a purple fill color and white font to the top 20% of the values in the range.

* * *

	A	B	C	D	E	F
1	Sample A	Sample B	Sample C	Sample D	Sample E	Sample F
2	1	✖	1	1	1	1
3	2	✖	2	2	2	2
4	3	✖	3	3	3	3
5	4	❗	4	4	4	4
6	5	❗	5	5	5	5
7	6	❗	6	6	6	6
8	7	❗	7	7	7	7
9	8	✔	8	8	8	8
10	9	✔	9	9	9	9
11	10	✔	10	10	10	10

Sample B: Use Conditional Formatting, Icon Sets, Indicators, and choose the 3 Symbols (Uncircled) option.

Then go to Manage Rules, choose the rule and Edit Rule, and click on the box for Show Icon Only.

Sample C: Use Conditional Formatting, Highlight Cells Rules, Between, enter 5 and 7, and then choose Custom Format. Choose the Blue standard color and Bold formatting.

Sample D: Use Conditional Formatting, Data Bars, Solid Fill. Then go to Manage Rules, choose the rule and Edit Rule, and set the Minimum Type to Number and 2 and the Maximum Type to Number and 8.

Sample E: Use Conditional Formatting, Color Scales, Green-White Color Scale. Then go to Manage Rules, choose the rule and Edit Rule, and change the color under Minimum to a light gold color and the color under Maximum to a dark gold color.

Sample F: Use Conditional Formatting, Top/Bottom Rules, Top 10%, change it to 20%, and then choose Custom Format. Go to the Fill tab and choose the purple color. Go to the Font tab and change the color in the dropdown to white. Click OK.

EXERCISE 3

Recreate the following table (formatting optional) and then provide answers to the questions below :

	A	B	C	D
1	**Customer**	**Date**	**Units**	**Product**
2	Jones	1/1/2018	5	Whatsit
3	Smith	1/2/2018	10	Whatsit
4	Baker	1/3/2018	25	Whatsit
5	Smith	1/4/2018	25	Thingy
6	Baker	1/5/2018	10	Thingy
7	Jones	1/6/2018	5	Thingy
8	Baker	1/7/2018	5	Whatsit
9	Jones	1/8/2018	5	Whatsit
10	Jones	1/9/2018	10	Whatsit
11				

1. How many total units has Customer Jones purchased?
2. How many Whatsits has Customer Baker purchased?
3. How many Thingies did Customer Smith purchase?

4. How many total units were purchased between January 1st and January 4th?

* * *

The easiest way to answer most of these questions is to create a pivot table with Customer in the Rows section, Product in the Columns section, and Sum of Units in the Values section. To answer the last question, add Date to the Filters section and check only the boxes for January 1st through 4th.

	A	B	C	D
1	Date	(Multiple Items)		
2				
3	Sum of Units	Product		
4	Customer	Thingy	Whatsit	Grand Total
5	Baker		25	25
6	Jones		5	5
7	Smith	25	10	35
8	Grand Total	25	40	65

Answers:
1. 25
2. 30
3. 25
4. 65

* * *

Another option is to apply filters to the data. For question 1 you could filter by customer name and then highlight Column C to see the sum of the values, for example.

You could also sort the data by customer name and then product type for the first few questions.

EXERCISE 4

Using the below data, create a stacked bar chart, a clustered column chart, and a line chart for the monthly entries and a pie chart using the YTD column.

For the line chart include a data table with legend keys and remove the legend.

For the bar chart change the default colors.

For the pie chart add labels that show the total value for each slice on the outside and explode the pie so that the slices are slightly separated.

	A	B	C	D	E	F	G	H
1		January	February	March	April	May	June	YTD
2	Alpha	15	20	25	30	35	40	165
3	Beta	25	23	21	19	17	15	120
4	Omega	10	20	10	20	10	20	90

* * *

For the bar, column, and line chart options highlight Cells A1 through G4, go to the Charts section of the Insert tab, and choose the desired chart type from the dropdowns for each chart type.

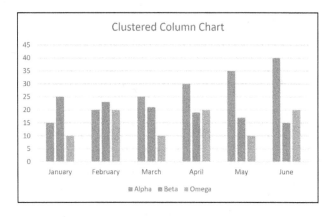

To add a data table and remove the legend from the line chart, click on the line chart and go to the Design tab under Chart Tools, click on Add Chart Element, and go to the Legend and Data Table options and make the appropriate selections.

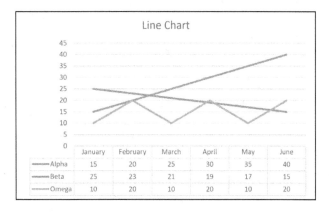

To change the colors in the bar chart, click on the chart. If Change Colors is available, you can choose from one of those options. Otherwise, click on each colored element in the chart, go to the Format tab under Chart Tools, and change the Shape Fill color for each one.

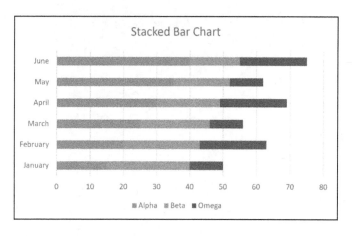

For the pie chart, highlight Cells A1 through A4 and H1 through H4, go to the Charts section of the Insert tab, and choose the 2-D pie chart option from the dropdowns for pie charts. To add labels to each slice, click on the chart and go to the Design tab under Chart Tools, click on Add Chart Element, and choose Data Labels and then Outside End. To explode the pie chart, click on the chart, go to Format Data Series on the right-hand side, click on Series Options at the top (the three bars), and explode the pie by about 7%.

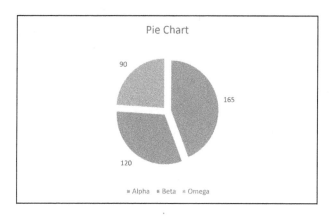

EXERCISE 5

Using the same data from Exercise 3, isolate a list of your unique customer names and write a function that will sum the total number of units each customer bought. Assume your data covers thousands of rows and that you may be dealing with hundreds of customer names.

	A	B	C	D
1	**Customer**	**Date**	**Units**	**Product**
2	Jones	1/1/2018	5	Whatsit
3	Smith	1/2/2018	10	Whatsit
4	Baker	1/3/2018	25	Whatsit
5	Smith	1/4/2018	25	Thingy
6	Baker	1/5/2018	10	Thingy
7	Jones	1/6/2018	5	Thingy
8	Baker	1/7/2018	5	Whatsit
9	Jones	1/8/2018	5	Whatsit
10	Jones	1/9/2018	10	Whatsit
11				

* * *

1. Copy your list of customer names from Column A to a new column that's separate from your existing data (in this case Column I) and remove duplicates from that column using Remove Duplicates from under the Data Tools section of the Data tab.

2. In the column next to that, in this case Column J, write a SUMIFS formula =SUMIFS(C:C,A:A,I2) which says to sum the number of units in Column C when the customer name in Column A is equal to the value in Cell I2 where the first of your list of unique customer names is.

3. Copy the SUMIFS formula from Cell J2 down as many rows as needed for all customer names in Column J.

INDEX OF QUIZZES

ABOUT THE AUTHOR

M.L. Humphrey is a former stockbroker with a degree in Economics from Stanford and an MBA from Wharton who has spent close to twenty years as a regulator and consultant in the financial services industry.

You can reach M.L. at mlhumphreywriter@gmail.com or at mlhumphrey.com.